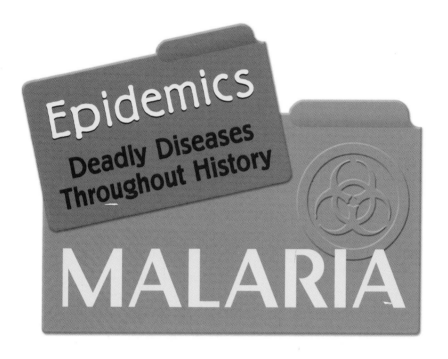

MICK ISLE

Epidemics
Deadly Diseases
Throughout History

MALARIA

The Rosen Publishing Group, Inc.
New York

To Helen, for putting malaria pills in our peanut butter sandwiches—and everything else.

Published in 2001 by The Rosen Publishing Group, Inc.
29 East 21st Street, New York, NY 10010

First Edition

Library of Congress Cataloging-in-Publication Data

Isle, Mick.
  Malaria / by Mick Isle—1st ed.
      p. cm. — (Epidemics)
Includes bibliographical references and index.
  ISBN 0-8239-3342-3
    1. Malaria—Juvenile literature. 2. Malaria—History—Juvenile literature. [1. Malaria. 2. Diseases. 3. Epidemics.]
I. Title. II. Series.
  RA644.M2 I754 2000
  616.9'362'009—dc21   00-009488

Cover image: This is a magnified image of red blood cells. The darker matter inside them is *Plasmodium vivax* malaria.

Manufactured in the United States of America

CONTENTS

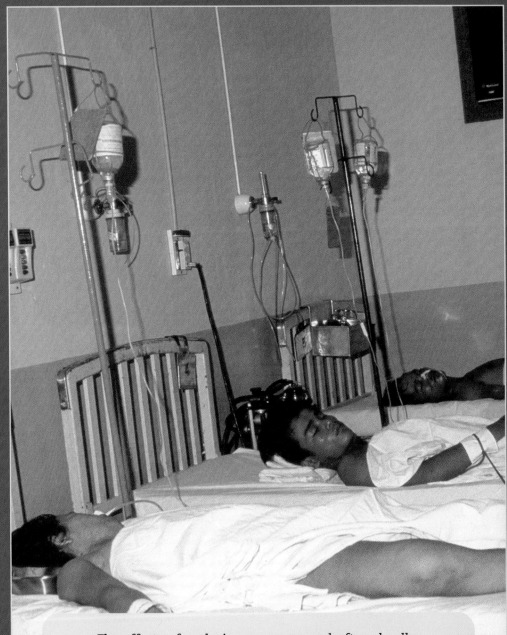

The effects of malaria are severe and often deadly.

INTRODUCTION

When I first arrived in Thailand, I spent some time in a remote village a friend had told me about. When I got there, the long rainy season was just beginning. According to the villagers, the rain brought two things: bananas and "forest fever." The village elders kindly warned me to stay away from bananas until the end of the rainy season. According to them, eating bananas brought on the deadly forest fever.

During my first few days, I counted close to one hundred children living in the village. Two weeks later, many of them had fallen ill. I saw a mother sob as her four-year-old son shook with violent *chills. It was as if instead of lying in his bed in the humid tropics, he was naked on an Arctic iceberg. I watched a grandmother place sooth-ing wet cloths across the forehead of her three-year-old granddaughter while rivers of sweat drenched the sheets she lay on. I saw another mother try to hold her young son down as his body went into violent convulsions that caused him to scream.*

In fact, many children cried out in pain. Others slipped into silent comas from which they never awoke. Afraid of falling ill myself, I left the village and continued my travels. Some months later, however, I returned to the village by chance. I was horrified to discover that in my absence twenty of the village children had died from the horrible forest fever.

Reading this passage from the diary of a young American traveling in Southeast Asia, you might be tempted to think of this strange illness as a mythical disease that affected people living in far-off lands, at another time. In actual fact, "forest fever" has another name: malaria. And you get it not by eating bananas, but by being bitten by one of many differ-ent kinds of female mosquitoes. As of yet, there is no surefire vaccine against malaria. And despite the efforts of researchers and doctors around the world, there is no foolproof way of getting rid of it.

The scary truth is that in tropical countries of Latin America, Asia, and particularly Africa, an estimated 300 million people are currently infected with malaria. Of these people, an estimated two to three million—most of whom are children under the age of five—will die from this deadly disease. And these statistics don't date from the last century, but from last year!

1

THE ORIGINS OF MALARIA

Have you ever thought about what would happen if a mysterious disease suddenly emerged and caused people to start dropping like flies? Picture, for instance, what would occur if all at once, 30 million Americans ceased to exist. The entire country would be turned upside-down. And it would stay upside-down for decades to come. If you think this sounds like a bad sci-fi movie, think again. At the beginning of the twentieth century, 30 million was the number of people who died worldwide—and quite horribly, too, coughing up and often choking on their own blood—during the Great Flu Epidemic of 1918. All of this occurred over a period of *four months*! The same number of people were killed during World War I—but in the space of *four years*!

How Epidemics Change History

An epidemic occurs when an infectious disease spreads beyond a local population and infects people throughout a vast region, over a long period of time. When an epidemic goes worldwide, affecting people all over the globe, it becomes a pandemic.

Before the arrival of the twentieth century, both epidemics and pandemics were leading causes of death. In fact, prior to World War I, if there was a war being waged, you were much more likely to die from an infectious disease spread by an enemy army than from the wounds inflicted by the guns and swords of that army.

When the Spanish conquistadors came to America, for instance, it wasn't with gunpowder that they killed off up to 90 percent of the native population and colonized most of Latin America. Instead, they spread deadly diseases—including malaria—to which American Indians had never been exposed. The few natives that survived were so impressed by the Christian god that seemed to protect European armies from such illnesses that they allowed themselves to be converted to Christianity. (In reality, Europeans were more resistant to these deadly diseases, having lived with them for centuries.)

As you can see, as a result of epidemic diseases, the entire history of the New World was completely

6000 BC
First written reference to deadly fevers thought to be malaria.

500 BC
Greek physician Hippocrates describes cyclical nature of malaria fevers and associates the disease with swamp water.

1500s
Malaria comes to America from infected European colonists and African slaves.

changed. And this is just one example of the impact epidemics can and have had on this planet.

Of course, it is one thing to open up a history book and read about how, in only two years' time, close to 40 percent of Europe's population collapsed and died of being infected with a virus. All of this because of a nasty illness called the bubonic plague. This happened in the fourteenth century—well before the discovery of much medical knowledge concerning the origin, means of transmission, treatment, prevention, and cure of many diseases. But it is much harder to believe that at the beginning of the twenty-first century—even in the industrialized world—epidemics can have such a big impact on our lives. Just look at

1630s
Jesuit missionaries in Peru learn from native people about the anti-malarial properties of the cinchona tree and introduce quinine, a powder made from the tree's bark, to Europe and Asia.

1717
Italian doctor Giovanni Maria Lancisi blames malaria on poisonous vapors released by swamp water.

1880
First true sighting of the malaria parasite by the French doctor Alphonse Laveran.

(continued)

the havoc a disease by the name of acquired immune deficiency syndrome (AIDS) has wreaked. Not only has AIDS killed millions of people and infected even more, it has also led to major transformations in sexual behavior and social attitudes.

The Oldest Disease in Existence

Of course, AIDS reared its ugly head only near the end of the twentieth century. Malaria has been around since day one—or at least since people first started taking notes on the strange and deadly fevers that caused entire populations to burn up and waste away (about 6000 BC). There are various references to

1897
British surgeon Ronald Ross cracks the mystery of how humans are infected by malaria via mosquitoes.

1898
Italian zoologist Giovanni Batista Grassi traces the course of plasmodium from human to mosquito to human and identifies the anopheles as the culprit.

1934
First synthetic version of quinine is manufactured in Germany.

1942
Invention of the insecticide DDT.

1961
First chloroquine resistant strains of *Plasmodium falciparum* are discovered in Thailand.

1967
WHO announces that global eradication of malaria is impossible and shifts its focus to controlling the disease.

1970s
Introduction of a completely synthesized form of quinine: mefloquine.

1943
American pharma-
ceutical company
launches
chloroquine.

1944
DDT is first used
in Italy.

1950
Launch of a
global project to
control malaria by
spraying DDT.

1950s
The World Health
Organization (WHO)
announces strategy for worldwide eradication of malaria.

1972
Global eradication
of malaria
program is
declared dead.

1987
Colombian
biochemist
Manuel Patarroyo
develops the first
vaccine against
the *Plasmodium
falciparum*
parasite.

When the Spanish conquistadors arrived in the New World,
they brought disease with them.

malaria-like diseases in the medical texts of many ancient civilizations. Apparently Babylonians, Egyptians, Indians, and Chinese all suffered from fatal fevers. Because it was generally believed that malaria was caused by some angry god or irritable divinity, the most popular cures included amulets and lucky charms, magic rituals, sacrifices, and special potions made from medicinal herbs.

By 1000 BC, outbreaks of malaria were already common in Mediterranean countries such as Greece. In fact, the Greek word for fever was almost always associated with malaria. In his influential writings, the famous Greek doctor Hippocrates (460-377 BC) was the first to identify the cycles of malarial fevers as well as the disease's link to the stagnant waters of swamps and marshes. In fact, Hippocrates believed that warm and humid weather in itself was very unhealthy. He held the weather directly responsible for many ailments, including malaria.

Some historians believe that malaria was partially to blame for the decline of Ancient Greece. They claim that the disease, responsible not only for many deaths but for the many citizens whose slow recoveries left them incapacitated, led to a weakened society. This in turn made it difficult to govern the country (rulers kept perishing), to defend it (fewer soldiers), and even to eat (many farms were abandoned).

Centuries later, when the Roman Empire fell into serious decline, malaria was once again a major factor. Although malaria had been around Ancient Rome for centuries, up until around 400 BC it appeared in only a mild form. However, changes in climate and the cutting down of forests for farmland (which, when abandoned, led to the formation of marshes) made the area much more inviting for tougher mosquitoes carrying stronger strains of malaria from Africa. The result was a series of major epidemics over a period of decades, which devastated Roman society.

During the centuries that followed—known as the Dark Ages—much of the medical knowledge the Greeks and Romans had gained about malaria was forgotten. Malaria itself lost its identity and became confused with other run-of-the-mill types of feverish illnesses. In the meantime,

Greek doctor Hippocrates (460-377 BC)

as sanitation methods used by the Greeks and Romans were neglected, the disease continued to spread through Europe. By the sixth century, people were coming down with malaria in England, France, Holland, and even as far north as Scandinavia.

At this point, malaria was blamed on angry gods bent on punishing humans and on supposedly weird alignments of certain heavenly stars and planets. It was thought that to cure malaria, you had to get rid of the bad "humors," which were bodily fluids associated with distinct moods and illnesses, that, in excess, could poison your body. You could do this by bleeding, or making cuts in your skin that would allow bad fluids to escape; by purging, which you did by drinking herbal potions that would cause you to vomit the bad stuff out of your system; and cauterization, which involved branding your skin with a hot iron.

By the twelfth century, malaria was common all over Europe. When, on the heels of Columbus, the first Spanish conquistadors arrived in the New World, the disease tagged along with them and spread throughout the Americas. In fact, the business of "discovering" and colonizing the world made it very easy for new strains of malaria to spread all over the globe, courtesy of European adventurers and their ships.

A FAMOUS DEATH BY MALARIA

Oliver Cromwell

You've probably heard of Oliver Cromwell. He led the New Model Army (nick-named the "Roundheads"), which in 1646 booted King Charles I out of England. Three years later, Charles I was beheaded and Cromwell became lord-general and commander-in-chief of the Commonwealth. In this new role, Cromwell repossessed farms and the estates of nobles in Ireland and turned them over to his loyal supporters. He sent an expedition across the Atlantic and took Jamaica from Spain in 1655. Over the next three years, Cromwell's health steadily declined, and he died of malaria in 1658.

Between the sixteenth century and the eighteenth century, malaria became endemic in most of Europe. A disease that is said to be endemic is one that is so common and widespread that it has become characteristic of a given area. Even though malaria became an ever present part of life in many areas, there were still numerous epidemics that broke out during this period. In 1602, for example, the disease struck down 40,000 people in Italy alone.

2

MALARIA IN MODERN TIMES

Although there were plenty of mosquitoes in the New World, according to the well-kept books of local civilizations such as the Mayas and Aztecs, there wasn't any sign of malaria until infected Europeans brought it with them when they crossed the ocean.

Malaria Comes to America

When the Indians of North and South America kept dying mysteriously, greedy European settlers started importing boatloads of slaves from Africa to work their vast sugarcane, tobacco, and cotton plantations. If Africans seemed sturdier and less vulnerable to malaria than Native Americans, it was undoubtedly

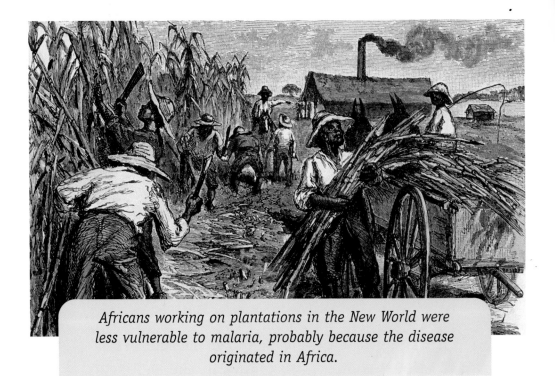

Africans working on plantations in the New World were less vulnerable to malaria, probably because the disease originated in Africa.

because malaria originated in Africa in the first place. Over the centuries, this had allowed Africans' immune systems to build up a natural resistance to the disease. Of course, when these slaves were transported across the ocean, they brought malaria along with them.

In the United States, malaria was already around when the first colonies were founded. In fact, it was present during numerous important occasions in American history. The disease quite literally played a part in American independence: One of the first military expenditures passed by Congress in 1775 was for $300 to buy quinine to protect General Washington's troops.

Funnily enough, while the rest of the world exported malaria to the Americas, it was in the Americas that the first cure for malaria was discovered and then exported to the rest of the world.

Long before the first Spanish conquistadors landed in South America, the Indians of Peru and Ecuador had already discovered a potent remedy against heavy-duty fevers. Quinine was made by drying and crushing the bark of the cinchona tree. According to legend, quinine was first brought to Europe in 1632 by the countess of Chinchon, wife

Scraping tree bark

of the viceroy of Peru. Although in actual fact the Countess died of malaria before ever reaching the Old World, for years after, this "miraculous" cure for malaria was known as "the countess's powder." It later came out that the medicine's true importer was an unknown Jesuit missionary who had been converting Indians in South America.

Quinine was an instant hit in Europe and was especially popular with Europe's royal families. Because so many kings and queens had died of malaria, many royals reached for quinine the minute their foreheads felt warm. In malaria-infested India, quinine became the rage as well, although in another form. Since tonic water contained quinine, the refreshing combination of gin and tonic became a classic anti-malaria cocktail among British colonial rulers.

Malaria affected between 50 and 80 percent of Union army soldiers during the Civil War.

Later, during the Civil War (1861-1865), between 50 and 80 percent of the soldiers in the Union army came down with the disease each year. In fact, for a long time, malaria was endemic in areas such as the Mississippi Valley and around the Chesapeake Bay.

Even chilly Canada was not safe from malaria. In the summer of 1828, "swamp fever" broke out in the village of Bytown (which later became the Canadian capital of Ottawa). It was believed to have been brought over by infected British soldiers who had been in the British colony of India. By the time the Canadian cold had killed off the mosquitoes in September, many people had already succumbed to what had quickly become an epidemic.

Outbreaks of malaria continued in the United States well into the 1940s. In 1914 alone, there were over 600,000 cases of malaria recorded in the United States. Although today it is quite rare, there are nonetheless close to 1,200 Americans who are infected with malaria each year, most while traveling abroad. There were recent cases of malaria in New York City in 1993 and in Michigan in 1995. Since the outbreaks were limited, mosquito-control efforts were not needed. But since malaria-carrying mosquitoes tend to spend their summers "vacationing" throughout most of the United States, the possibility of the disease reestablishing itself is a possibility.

Malaria was especially widespread in Brazil, with its warm climate and abundant jungles, swamps, and rivers. For over four centuries, Brazil experienced major malaria epidemics. Until the end of the nineteenth century, there were various beliefs about what caused the deadly disease. One supposed source was the effect of the sun's heat on stagnant water. The resulting evaporation was thought to release poisonous vapors into the air. (Lightning from frequent storms was thought to zap the deadly vapors away.) Other supposed malaria sources ranged from overeating to undercooking meat to drinking well water to sucking oranges at night.

Equally varied were the means of curing these "bad tempered" fevers. Although quinine was available early on, the problem was that overdosing on quinine over a long period could lead to temporary deafness, dizziness, or a ringing in the ears. There were other methods, however. In 1883, the sister of Emperor Pedro II of Brazil, Princess Paula Mariana, came down with a bad case of malaria. The royal doctors not only made her take quinine both orally and anally, they also stuffed her with soups and applied bloodsucking leeches, mustard plaster, and burning chemicals to her skin. Not surprisingly, all of this made the poor ten-year-old princess scream out in pain.

Throughout the twentieth century, Brazil has continued to experience malaria epidemics. By the latter part of the century, however, the cases had become confined to poorer, damper, and more isolated northern regions, particularly those closest to the Amazon. Nonetheless, Brazil today still has the greatest percentage of all malaria cases reported in the Americas—56 percent.

Meanwhile, in the more tropical climes of South and Central America, malaria-carrying mosquitoes have been even more active over the years. From the sixteenth century on, malaria was endemic in much of Latin America.

Malaria in the World Today

After years of decline, malaria is once again on the move. Despite the media attention given to AIDS and the Ebola virus, malaria wipes out millions every year. It is a public health problem in some ninety countries worldwide. This puts two billion people at risk—36 percent of the world's population. According to estimates made by the World Health Organization (WHO), malaria infects about 400 million people each year. Of these, close to 90 percent live in Africa.

Although malaria is a risk in various regions of Asia and Latin America (mainly in India, Afghanistan, Sri Lanka, Thailand, Indonesia, Cambodia, Vietnam, China, and Brazil), Africa is unlucky enough to be the main target of the devastation caused by the disease. It is estimated that an average African receives 40 to 120 infective mosquito bites a year. As a result, an estimated 1.5 million Africans die from malaria each year. The majority of these are young children who live in rural areas with few health services. In Africa, malaria is responsible for one-third of all hospital admissions and one-quarter of all deaths of children under the age of five. It is also responsible, in many ways, for such widespread poverty. It is estimated that one case of malaria results in the loss of ten working days a year. Furthermore, the total cost spent on treating malaria in Africa per year is around $2 billion. Because the situation seems only to be getting worse, the WHO has declared malaria control to be a top global priority.

3

THE WAY MALARIA WORKS

There are three factors responsible for the spread of malaria: parasites, mosquitoes, and human beings. Interestingly, after centuries of wreaking epidemic havoc, it was only at the end of the 1800s that these three culprits were finally unmasked.

The Parasite

"Parasite" doesn't just mean a moocher who sponges off other people. In nature, a parasite is a creature or organism that lives on or inside another creature (which is sort of like mooching in a way). The malaria parasite is a tiny thing that goes by the name of plasmodium. Although almost all mammals can be infected by plasmodium parasites, different animal species can be infected only by their own particular species of the parasite. Humans, for example, can't get malaria from the same kind of parasites that infect monkeys, birds, or snakes. To date there are four species of malaria parasites that are known to make people sick: *Plasmodium falciparum, Plasmodium vivax, Plasmodium ovale,* and *Plasmodium malariae.* The most deadly of all is *Plasmodium falciparum,* which can cause lethal complications such as cerebral (brain) malaria.

The first sighting of a malaria parasite was made in 1880 by Alphonse Laveran, a French army surgeon working in Algeria, who detected the parasite while looking through a microscope at the blood of a malaria patient. Initially, the medical community rejected Laveran's discovery. It was only in 1886 that Italian scientists (due to the many malaria epidemics in Italy, Italians were the leading specialists) officially recognized the parasite as the source of the disease. However, another big mystery remained to be solved: How did the parasite infect humans?

The Mosquito

The big answer turned out to be via mosquitoes. For quite some time, mosquitoes had been suspects: As early as 1717, an Italian doctor named Giovanni Maria Lancisi suggested mosquitoes' involvement in the spread of malaria. However, they weren't proven guilty until much later. In fact, it was not until 1897 that the riddle was solved by Ronald Ross, a British army physician.

As both Ross and Italian zoologist Giovanni Batista Grassi discovered, not just any old mosquito can be a carrier of human malaria. The culprit was proven to be a striped-winged mosquito belonging to the *Anopheles* genus. Female anopheles need human blood to provide energy for the eggs they lay. Because of this, when evening comes around— this is their favorite feeding time—the ladies go hunting. Not only can they see you and smell you (from up to sixty feet away), but they can also detect the radiation

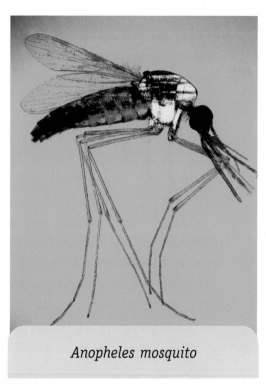

Anopheles mosquito

given off by your warm body. Once they have tracked you down, the hungry females get to work sucking blood from their human hosts. If the host in question happens to be infected with a malaria parasite, this gets sucked up as well.

Surgeon Ronald Ross (1857-1932) was intent on solving the mystery of malaria when he was stationed in malaria-infested India. In 1894, during a trip to London, Ross looked up a colleague named Patrick Manson. While working in China, Manson had discovered that when mosquitoes fed on blood from animals, they also sucked up parasites before passing them along to their next meal. Could this be the key to the spread of malaria? Intrigued by the possibility, Ross returned to India determined to test out this idea.

After two years of experiments, on August 20, 1897, (which he later called "Mosquito Day"), Ross found a human malaria parasite in the stomach of a mosquito that had fed on a malaria patient. He was so excited by his discovery that he wrote a poem predicting mosquitoes' eventual day of reckoning.

Unfortunately, Ross was unable to prove the entire sequence of infection using human guinea pigs. In 1898, he was able to show how a mosquito that had fed on a bird with malaria spread the disease to a healthy bird by biting this new bird. However, at this time in Rome, the Italian zoologist Giovanni Batista Grassi beat him to the punch. Carrying out the same experiment with mosquitoes and humans, Grassi succeeded in confirming how human malaria was spread.

In spite of this setback, Ross dedicated the rest of his life to finding ways of preventing the spread of the disease. His efforts were rewarded when he won a Nobel Prize for medicine in 1902.

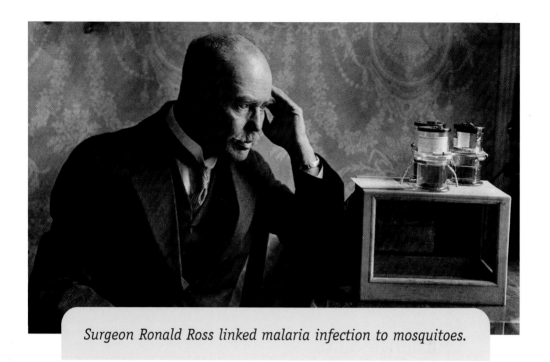

Surgeon Ronald Ross linked malaria infection to mosquitoes.

Inside the mosquito, the parasite spends two to three weeks going through a period of complex changes. During this time it becomes infectious. It then moves up to the mosquito's saliva glands, where it lies, ready and waiting, for the bug to bite its next human victim.

When you are bitten by an infected anopheles, the parasite then moves in and infects you. Once inside of you, the threadlike parasite enters your bloodstream and is carried to your liver, where it begins reproducing like crazy. New offspring are then rereleased into the bloodstream where they attack and destroy the red blood cells, which carry oxygen throughout your body. From time to time, a new form of the parasite bursts forth from the destroyed blood cells and travels through your bloodstream invading new blood cells. Such bursts are responsible for the peaks of malarial fever that victims experience. The four different malaria parasites produce different fever cycles in which fever rises, falls, and rises again. *Plasmodium falciparum,* for example, has a forty-eight-hour period between fever peaks. In a malaria patient, these cycles of attacks and fevers continue over and over until natural or acquired immunity, antimalarial remedies, or death bring the repetitive process to an end.

MOSQUITO FACTS

- There are about 2,700 different species of these pesky bugs.

- The average mosquito weighs 2 to 2.5 milligrams.

- Male mosquitoes don't suck blood—only females do it (an average drink is five-millionths of a liter).

- If the sensory nerve in a mosquito's stomach is cut, it will keep sucking blood until it bursts.

- Mosquitoes whiz around at the speed of around one mile an hour.

- Although some mosquitoes can travel distances of up to 100 miles, most fly within a radius of only one mile throughout their entire lifetimes.

- In warm weather, mosquitoes can produce a new generation in a mere week.

Although anopheles rarely fly more than a couple of miles from their homes, they have been known to hitch rides on airplanes and high-speed ships. In 1928, a French ship carrying mail from western Africa to northern Brazil also carried along an African variety of anopheles that until then had been unknown in South America. The imported mosquito turned out to be much more efficient at spreading malaria than its Brazilian cousin. In no time, Brazil was in the throes of the worst epidemic it had ever experienced. Deaths were so plentiful that entire districts were wiped out.

Because of such "accidents," international law requires disinsectization of all aircrafts and ships prior to their departure and enforces rigid antimosquito sanitation in all ports and airports.

Although anopheles inhabit tropical regions—neither the mosquitoes nor their parasitic guests can survive cold temperatures (anything below fifteen degrees Celsius, or fifty-nine degrees Fahrenheit, is fatal to both)—very few malarial *anopheles* hang out in tropical forests. This is because female mosquitoes lay their eggs to hatch in small, sunlit areas of water. Dense tropical jungles tend to be pretty dark. So mosquitoes like it when humans come along and, for whatever reason, clear farmland or cut down forests. The treeless land provides mosquitoes with both the ideal conditions and the proximity to human hosts that they require to reproduce. Since from the

Some man-made conditions where malaria can thrive include deforested areas, sewage facilities, dams, and on irrigated land.

beginning of civilization humans have been quite happy to hack down forests, over the centuries both mosquitoes and malaria have thrived. More recently, irrigation projects, dams, and improper sewage systems in overcrowded city slums have done much to increase the explosion of "man-made" malaria.

Humans

As we have seen, human beings are the source of the malaria parasites that infect other humans. If malaria-bearing mosquitoes don't stray far from home, however, the same cannot be said of malaria-carrying humans. Over time, invading armies, explorers and traders, colonists and settlers, immigrants and refugees all played their parts in spreading malaria around the world. During World War II alone, over 500,000 American soldiers were interned for malaria caught overseas. And today, with increased travel to far-flung destinations, many North American tourists have returned to their malaria-free hometowns from a trip to the tropics, carrying the parasite with them.

In Africa, where the situation is extreme, there are many regions in which malaria is endemic. As a result of being bitten and rebitten, infected and reinfected throughout their lives, many Africans build up immunity to the disease. This means that although the plasmodium parasites might live within them throughout their lives, they will either suffer from mild symptoms from time to time or not experience any symptoms at all. In such endemic areas, children are protected in their first months of life by the disease-fighting antibodies produced by their immune mothers. After that, if they don't die from the disease (and, tragically, many do), they develop their own immunity over the years.

This immunity doesn't last forever, however. Completely immune adults who leave endemic regions will lose their immunity over a period of one to two years. Yet even if they have no outward symptoms, those who leave endemic regions carry the infection within them and can end up causing epidemics in areas where malaria had previously been under control. Similarly, migrants, refugees, and travelers who pass through endemic areas can quickly become infected. And so the cycle continues.

4

SYMPTOMS, DIAGNOSIS, PREVENTION, AND TREATMENTS

One evening, I received a call to examine a woman who was a friend of mine. Rita had been in a coma since that morning. Only the day before I had eaten lunch with her and she had told me that she was feeling tired. She chalked it up to her pregnancy. Or perhaps she had the beginnings of the flu. But when I arrived at the clinic, the interns had already started treating Rita for malaria. This in spite of the fact that two blood smears had shown no signs of the plasmodium parasite.

I quickly began looking for other possible infections, but her only symptoms

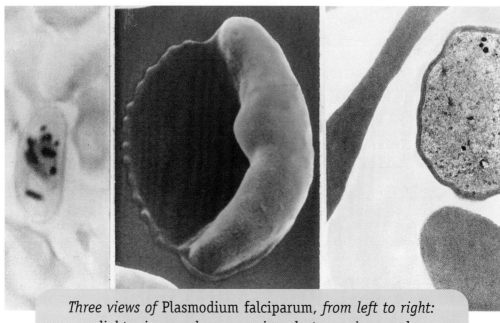

Three views of Plasmodium falciparum, *from left to right: a light micrograph, a scanning electron micrograph, and a transmission electron micrograph.*

were a high temperature and a deep coma. Although we continued to give her quinine, Rita's situation didn't improve. Two new blood smears showed no sign of plasmodium parasites. In the meantime, I tried to make sure that Rita didn't choke on her own vomit.

Rita's children arrived at the clinic. They had spent the day desperately trying to scrounge up money from friends and relatives so that Rita could be taken by truck to the town hospital, seventy miles away. The youngest children were crying. Their father had died from malaria only a few months before.

Just before we put Rita in the truck, I took two more smears. This time both slides showed a few Plasmodium falciparum *parasites wriggling around.*

Three days later, Rita was back at work. When I asked about her unborn baby, she looked away. The doctors at the hospital had told her she was lucky to be alive. Her baby hadn't been so lucky.

When news of Rita's miscarriage spread throughout the small village, a group of pregnant women came to the clinic. They were worried they would catch malaria and their babies would die, too. Although the safest malarial preventive for pregnant women—a drug called proguanil— works in only 50 percent of cases, I gave some to all the women and told them to call me immediately if they felt "the flu" coming on.

—from the notebook of a Canadian doctor
working in Africa

Getting Malaria

Once you are bitten by an infected anopheles, the plasmodium parasite will take a while to make its effects known. Depending on the plasmodium in question, this can range from between nine days *(plasmodium falciparum)* to thirty days *(Plasmodium malariae)*. Some strains of *Plasmodium vivax* might take up to nine months before they start doing their dirty work.

The first sign you might have malaria is if you suddenly break out in a fever. At first this might seem to be the flu. But if you have the slightest doubt, check it out. Most deaths are due to uncomplicated attacks of *Plasmodium falciparum* that, left unchecked, lead to severe cases.

Aside from fevers that come and go, other signs of malaria include headaches, aches and pains all over, diarrhea, shaking chills, sweating, and abdominal pains. If left untreated, malaria will leave you weak, groggy, and with yellowish skin. As the parasites increasingly clog up your bloodstream, the disease can lead to vomiting and convulsions, and, finally, kidney failure and/or cerebral malaria (in which you fall into a coma from which you will never awaken). Needless to say, both of these extreme conditions spell death.

Meanwhile, the jury is still out as to whether the pesky parasites cause mosquitoes as much harm as they do humans. It is generally believed that malaria-carrying mosquitoes *do* live shorter lives than their noninfected winged counterparts.

- Stay away from risky, endemic regions (check with the Centers for Disease Control).

- Try to travel after peak mosquito season (when it's cold).

- Mosquitoes don't like the daytime, since the hot sun tends to dry them out. Instead, they tend to whiz around at dusk and dawn (when their animal prey is most active). When they are outside, stay inside.

- Make sure your living quarters have screens on the windows and doors.

- Sleep under a mosquito net (without holes, and if possible, soaked in insecticide).

- Use mosquito repellents such as DEET.

- Soak your clothing in an insecticide called permethrin. One treatment will stay on through several washings.

- Wear long-sleeved clothing and long pants. Avoid dark colors, which mosquitoes love.

- Put up either a bat house or a house for purple martins. Both of these winged creatures love mosquitoes and gobble up hundreds every hour.

Preventing Malaria

Since there is no vaccine against it and no surefire cure for it, the best way to treat malaria is not to get it, or let it (or rather the mosquitoes that carry it) get you.

Many of the ways to avoid getting malaria are cheap, easy, and require little more than common sense. If you are going to a tropical area where malaria is a problem, see your doctor six weeks before your trip and get him or her to prescribe an antimalarial drug. The kind of antimalarial your doctor will prescribe depends on any medical conditions you might have and where you are traveling.

When you begin taking your medication, follow the instructions exactly. An overdose of antimalarials can be fatal. The following are the most commonly prescribed antimalarials:

- mefloquine
- chloroquine
- hydroxychloroquine sulfate
- doxycycline
- proguanil

All of these medications have potential side effects—ranging from nausea and headaches to

Sleeping under mosquito netting is a preventative measure against malaria.

dizziness and blurred vision. For this reason it is best to take them on a full stomach. You usually must continue taking these medications for several weeks after you have left a malarial region.

All of these antimalarials are *preventive* medications. They do not guarantee 100 percent protection. In fact, the bad news is that in many tropical regions, most particularly Southeast Asia, parasites are becoming increasingly resistant to many antimalarials.

Diagnosing Malaria

Diagnosing malaria properly and quickly is key to staying alive. If you have been in an area with malaria and if, even a year later, you are experiencing any of the symptoms previously mentioned, see a doctor *immediately*. Because early flulike symptoms can resemble one of many other diseases, including typhoid and meningitis, your doctor will need to take a blood sample. If you do have malaria, the parasites will show up—if not right away, then soon enough—under the microscope, swimming around in your red blood cells.

Treating Malaria

If you do come down with a case of malaria, you will most likely be treated with antimalarial drugs. These

In the mid-1800s, savvy Dutch colonists bought cinchona seeds from a British trader who had visited Peru. Looking to make some money, they established cinchona plantations in the Dutch colony of Java (today Indonesia) and soon had a monopoly on quinine. Things got tough, however, when during World War II the Japanese invaded Java. Suddenly the Allies were out of quinine. And there was a lot of malaria being spread around by traveling troops (including among many Americans).

This lack led scientists to put their heads together to come up with a synthesized version of the botanical drug, made from chemicals. The first attempts at manufacturing quinine had been by a German pharmaceutical company in 1934. But a more successful version was launched by Americans in 1943. This manufactured antimalarial was named chloroquine, and it would become the number one treatment for malaria. Later, during the Vietnam War, a completely synthesized version of quinine was invented called mefloquine.

Drying cinchona bark

will be administered first intravenously (through your veins) and then orally. Chloroquine is the antimalarial most commonly used, but in areas where the plasmodium parasite is resistant to this drug, doctors often prescribe good old quinine (often accompanied by antibiotics) in one of its many forms.

5

THE FUTURE OF MALARIA

Following World War II, for a while it seemed as if malaria might be licked once and for all. Two big discoveries in particular led the medical community to believe in such a miracle. One was the invention of chloroquine, which became a cheap and efficient way of nipping malaria parasites in the bud. The other was the invention and mass utilization of a deadly insecticide known as DDT (Dichloro-Dyphenyl-Trichloroethene), which became a cheap and efficient way of exterminating parasite-carrying mosquitoes.

In the late 1940s, the world went to war against malaria, and for a while it seemed to be winning. The global effort to do away with the disease included widespread spraying of favorite mosquito haunts with DDT; coating marshes with

Marshes were once sprayed with DDT to control the spread of malaria.

paraffin (a waxy substance used for sealing and coating that also prevents mosquito larvae from breathing); and draining stagnant water. These measures, coupled with the widespread use of chloroquine, had impressive results. In countries such as Italy, Hungary, Spain, Portugal, Korea, and the United States, malaria was wiped out for good. And in others, at least until the end of the 1960s, malaria was definitely on the wane.

However, in many tropical nations, Mother Nature's perverse ways, coupled with environmental disturbances and reduced government budgets combined forces to foil the WHO's plan to completely eradicate malaria once and for all.

FOUR REASONS MALARIA COULDN'T BE LICKED

1. Even as scientists began discovering the poisonous effect of DDT on friendly birds and bugs, not to mention humans who ate DDT-sprayed fruits, rougher and tougher anopheles mosquitoes had already built up resistance to the toxic spray.

2. Malaria parasites became resistance to chloroquine and then to other, newer antimalarials such as mefloquine.

3. Increased travel and international trade sent drug-resistant parasites all over the globe.

(continued)

4. Tougher and more widespread efforts to fight malaria grew more and more expensive. Many governments in poorer countries of Africa, Latin America, and Southeast Asia couldn't afford to pay for the health, education, and agricultural programs needed to control the disease.

The upshot of all this is that since the early 1970s the number of people infected by malaria around the world has more than tripled. And malaria is not only a "Third World" problem. Increasingly tough parasites and mosquitoes coupled with increasing travel has meant a rise in malaria cases in places where malaria was once extremely rare—places such as Europe and North America. Indeed, today the scientific community is less concerned with grandiose dreams of completely doing away with the disease and more bent on coming up with practical ways of controlling and reducing it.

Controlling Parasites

As plasmodium parasites become increasingly resistant to traditional antimalarials, instead of upping the dosages—which proves expensive and can create serious side effects—researchers are looking for completely new alternatives. One very promising alternative is in fact not so new at all. Derived from

*Loading docks can be breeding grounds for malaria
and other diseases.*

a family of plants known as artemisnins, Quinghaosu has been used medicinally to fight malarial fevers in China for over 2,000 years. Lately, the rest of the world has caught on, and tests have proved promising. Although not widely available, at this stage in the game artemisnins are the most effective antimalarials around, acting rapidly and with few side effects.

Meanwhile, research is underway to create a malaria vaccine. So far, the most promising is one developed by Dr. Manuel Patarroyo of Colombia. Although in test trials in Africa the vaccine prevented only 30 percent of deaths from malaria, supporters argue that 30 percent of three million deaths per year is better than none.

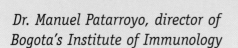

Dr. Manuel Patarroyo, director of Bogota's Institute of Immunology

Controlling Mosquitoes

Fearing that sooner or later plasmodium parasites will become resistant to artemisnins, many antimalarial

DDT and other pesticides can be harmful to the environment.

campaigns have been directed at getting rid of anopheles. Although mosquito specialists now believe that wiping out mosquitoes isn't realistic, certain steps can be taken to put a severe damper on their human-chomping activities.

DDT and other insecticides have proved problematic because not only do mosquitoes develop immunity to them, but the chemicals are environmentally unfriendly. So instead of chemical controls, scientists are currently looking at biological controls. Currently being explored are ways of getting other living organisms to eat or harm mosquitoes before mosquitoes eat or harm you. Such organisms include:

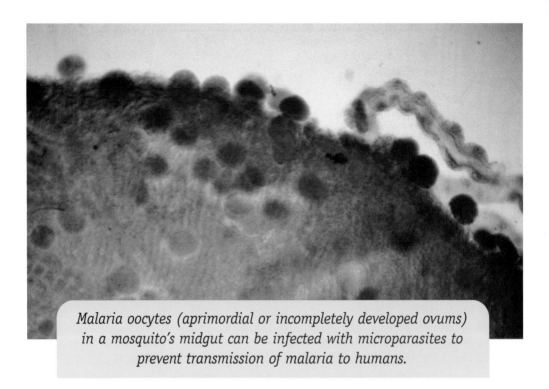

Malaria oocytes (aprimordial or incompletely developed ovums) in a mosquito's midgut can be infected with microparasites to prevent transmission of malaria to humans.

- ⊛ A microparasite discovered in Thailand that, when injected into a female mosquito, lives inside her stomach and infects her eggs. This creates a sluggish female mosquito with little energy left to bite humans.

- ⊛ A fungus, used to control mosquitoes on California farms, is already approved to be used in pastures and rice fields.

- ⊛ A blue-green algae that, if its degree of toxicity could be increased, would make hamburger meat out of the winged whiners.

In the meantime, while all the great ideas above are still in the developmental stage, health experts

Cleopatra wasn't the last African monarch to sleep under a mosquito net. King Gbaguidi XII, who rules a small kingdom in the West African country of Benin, now sleeps under one, too. Although Benin is prime malaria country, it was found that only 15 percent of the population was using mosquito nets. Researchers from Benin and Canada set to work to find out why.

Some people weren't aware that mosquitoes caused malaria. Quite a few associated malaria with getting too much sun, eating too many peanuts, or using too much red palm oil. Others found the heavy fabric of mosquito nets stiflingly hot at night. Finally, people didn't realize how much cheaper a mosquito net dipped in insecticide was compared to the cost of antimalarial medicine.

In similar studies carried out in other African countries, a certain number of families were given treated mosquito nets to use over a period of six months. Others were not. Over that half-year period, the families that used the nets had 50 percent fewer cases of malaria than those who didn't. In the end, everyone wanted mosquito nets.

King Gbaguidi XII is converted. "Before, I used to scratch myself and I had to go to the hospital. Now, I sleep very well. I don't feel a thing," confessed the king.

have come up with a much simpler, cheaper, and hands-on technique of keeping malaria at bay: using a good, old-fashioned mosquito net soaked in insecticide. After all, it was good enough for Cleopatra!

GLOSSARY

antibodies Proteins produced by your immune
system that attack foreign viruses and bacteria.

antimalarial Medicine used to fight the
malaria parasite.

contagious Disease that is spread by coming into
contact with someone who has the disease.

diagnosis Identification of a disease based on
signs and symptoms.

endemic Native to a particular people or country.

epidemic When an infectious disease spreads
beyond a local population and infects many more
people throughout a region.

eradicate To get rid of completely.

host Plant or animal that provides housing and
food for a parasite.

immunity Ability to resist a particular disease.

pandemic   Uncontrolled outbreak of an infectious disease on a global scale.

parasite   Creature or organism that lives on or inside another creature.

quinine   First cure for malaria, made from the dried crushed bark of the cinchona tree.

side effects   Secondary or adverse reactions to taking drugs or medications.

symptom   Sign or characteristic of a disease that can be felt (fever, chills, swelling) by a patient.

synthesis   Production of a substance by combining different chemical elements.

FOR MORE INFORMATION

In the United States

Centers for Disease Control and Prevention (CDC)
1600 Clifton Road
Atlanta, GA 30333
(404) 639-3534
(800) 311-3435
Web site: http://www.cdc.gov/travel/malinfo.htm

World Health Organization (WHO)
Regional Office for the Americas
525 23rd Street NW
Washington, DC 20037
(202) 974-3000
Web site: http://www.who.int

In Canada

Clinical Trials Research Center
Dalhousie University Department of Pediatrics
Halifax, Nova Scotia B3H 3J5
(902) 428-8992
Web site: http://www.dal.ca/~ctrc

Health Canada Laboratory Centre for Disease Control
Tunney's Pasture
AL 0913A
Ottawa, ON K1A 0K9
(613) 957-2991
Web site: http://www.hc-sc.gc.ca

Web Sites

Due to the changing nature of Internet links, the Rosen Publishing Group, Inc., has developed an online list of Web sites related to the subject of this book. This site is updated regularly. Please use this link to access the list:

http://www.rosenlinks.com/epid/mala

FOR FURTHER READING

Bray, R. S. *Armies of Pestilence—The Effects of Pandemics on History.* Jersey City, NJ: Parkwest Publications, 1998.

Bwire, Robert. *Bugs in Armor: A Tale of Malaria and Soldiering.* Foster City, CA: IUniverse.com., 1999.

Desowitz, Robert S. *The Malaria Capers: Tales of Parasites and People.* New York: W.W. Norton & Company, 1993.

Gibson, Mary E., and Edwin R. Nye. *Ronald Ross: Malariologist and Polymath: A Biography.* New York: St. Martin's Press, 1997.

Karlen, Arno. *Man and Microbes: Disease and Plagues in History and Modern Times.* New York: Simon and Schuster, 1996.

Lampton, Christopher F. *Epidemic* (A Disaster! Book). Brookfield, CT: Millbrook Press, 1994.

Poser, Charles M., and G. W. Bruyn. *An Illustrated History of Malaria.* Pearl River, NY: Parthenon Publishing, 1999.

Watts, Sheldon. *Epidemics and History: Disease, Power and Imperialism.* New Haven, CT: Yale University Press, 1998.

Yancey, Diane. *The Hunt for Hidden Killers—Ten Cases of Medical Mystery.* Brookfield, CT: Millbrook Press, 1994.

INDEX

CREDITS

About the Author

Mick Isle has a degree in journalism from Trinity College in Dublin, Ireland.

Photo Credits

Cover © Custom Medical Stock Photo/J.L. Carson; p. 4 © Sue Ford/Science Photo Library; pp. 14, 16, 20, and 22 © North Wind Pictures; p. 18 © Bettmann/CORBIS; pp. 21, 31, and 45 © Hulton-Deutsch Collection/CORBIS; p. 29 © Alfred Pasieka/Peter Arnold, Inc.; p. 34, upper left © Denise Deluise/Uniphoto; p. 34, other photos © Superstock; p. 38 © Custom Medical Stock Photo/Robert Becker, Ph.D.; p. 43 © David Samuel Robbins/CORBIS; p. 48 © CORBIS; p. 51 © Pictor; p. 52 © Associated Press (AP); p. 53 © Galen Rowell/CORBIS; p. 54 © Custom Medical Stock Photo/National Medical Slide Bank.

Design and Layout

Evelyn Horovicz